MEDITATIVE PHOTOGRAPHY

Discovering Mindfulness through Photography

IV
INVALER PRINT

Specializing in lifestyle books, that cover a wide range of topics, with the aim to provide readers with practical and inspiring information to help lead a fulfilling and enjoyable life.

2023 Invaler Print

First Published in 2023 by Invaler Print.

ISBN: 9798396037410

Design: Skip Armstrong
Front Cover and Back Cover Images: Skip Armstrong
Page Layout: Skip Armstrong

Description: Introducing "Meditative Photography - Learning Mindfulness Through Photography," a comprehensive guidebook that unveils the profound connection between mindfulness and the art of photography. Authored by a renowned photographer and mindfulness practitioner, this book is your key to unlocking inner peace and creative awareness through the transformative practice of Meditative Photography.

A message from the author, Skip Armstrong: Shoutout to you. Yeah, you! You're reading the "fine print". I appreciate you, and wish you the best. If you enjoy this book, please leave a good review and share it with someone you love. Your good word means the world to me.

Dedicated to Paul

6

Table of Contents

10

Photography as Meditation

Photography has the potential to be a powerful form of meditation, providing a pathway to mindfulness, introspection, and a deeper connection with the present moment. By immersing oneself in the act of capturing images and focusing solely on the process, photographers can transform their practice into a meditative experience.

To make photography a meditative practice, it is important to cultivate a mindset of mindfulness. Before beginning a photography session, take a few moments to center yourself and let go of distractions. By grounding yourself in the present moment, you can fully engage with your surroundings and approach photography with a heightened sense of awareness.

Slowing down and observing becomes a fundamental aspect of photography as a meditative practice. Rather than rushing to capture as many images as possible, take the time to truly see and connect with your subject. Pay attention to the interplay of light and shadow, the intricate details, and the unique moments that unfold before your lens. By immersing yourself in the present moment, you can capture images that reflect a deeper appreciation and understanding of the subject matter.

Patience is a virtue when it comes to making photography a meditative practice. Allow yourself to wait for the perfect moment, be it the right light, a spontaneous expression, or a captivating composition. Patience allows you to cultivate a state of receptivity and surrender, embracing the ebb and flow of the creative process. By embracing patience, you develop a greater capacity for capturing images that evoke emotions and tell meaningful stories.

Connecting with your subject on a deeper level is another key aspect of photography as a meditative practice. Whether photographing landscapes, people, or objects, take the time to establish a genuine connection. Engage with the energy, emotions, or essence of your subject. This connection allows you to capture images that not only visually resonate but also evoke a sense of presence and intimacy.

Simplification and focus are essential in creating a meditative photography practice. In a world filled with distractions, it is crucial to strip away unnecessary elements and concentrate on the core essence of your subject. By simplifying your composition and eliminating distractions, you create space for a more profound and impactful image.

Let go of expectations and attachments to the outcome. Instead of fixating on the end result, focus on the process of capturing images. Embrace the inherent imperfections and unpredictability of the moment. By letting go of preconceived notions, you open yourself up to the beauty of serendipity and the magic of the unexpected.

Photography can serve as a powerful form of meditation. By adopting a mindful approach, cultivating patience, connecting with your subjects, simplifying your vision, and letting go of expectations, you can transform the act of capturing images into a deeply meditative and introspective practice. Through photography, you have the opportunity to immerse yourself fully in the present moment, discover new perspectives, and find a sense of peace and tranquility.

14

Focus on the Present

Being fully present in the act of capturing each photograph and immersing yourself in the beauty of the environment is crucial for creating meaningful and impactful images. By cultivating a deep sense of presence and connecting with the surroundings, photographers can capture the essence and emotions of a moment with authenticity and depth.

To be fully present, it is essential to let go of distractions and quiet the mind. Take a few moments before starting your photography session to center yourself. Breathe deeply, grounding yourself in the present moment. Release any thoughts or concerns that may be pulling your attention away from the beauty of the environment. By quieting the mind, you create space to fully engage with your surroundings.

Immersing yourself in the beauty of the environment requires a keen awareness of the details and elements that make a scene captivating. Slow down and observe the interplay of light and shadow, the textures, the colors, and the composition. By taking the time to truly see, you can capture images that convey the atmosphere and evoke emotions.

Engage your senses fully to enhance your experience. Listen to the sounds of nature, the laughter of people, or the quiet whispers of a moment. Feel the textures beneath your fingertips or the breeze on your skin. By involving all your senses, you deepen your connection with the environment and enrich your perception of the moment you are capturing.

Let go of preconceived notions and open yourself up to spontaneity and serendipity. Embrace the unexpected and allow yourself to be surprised by what unfolds before your lens. This mindset of openness and flexibility allows you to capture unique and authentic moments that may have otherwise gone unnoticed.

Practice gratitude for the opportunity to be in such a beautiful environment and to witness the wonders around you. Cultivating gratitude shifts your perspective and enhances your ability to see the beauty in the smallest of details. It allows you to approach each photograph with a sense of reverence and appreciation, leading to images that are imbued with a deep sense of gratitude.

Maintaining a state of curiosity and wonder is also vital in being fully present and immersing yourself in the beauty of the environment. Approach each scene with a childlike curiosity, eager to discover new angles, perspectives, and hidden gems. Allow yourself to be captivated by the intricacies and magic of the world around you.

Remember to enjoy the process and find joy in the act of capturing each photograph. Photography is not just about the final image; it is about the journey and the experience of being present in the moment. Let the act of photographing become a form of meditation, a way to connect with your surroundings and express your creative vision.

Being fully present in the act of capturing each photograph and immersing yourself in the beauty of the environment requires a conscious effort to quiet the mind, observe, engage the senses, let go of expectations, practice gratitude, and cultivate curiosity. By doing so, you create a space for profound connection, authenticity, and creativity, resulting in images that reflect the true essence and beauty of the environment.

Observe Mindfully

Photographing with mindfulness entails paying attention to the details and observing your surroundings with heightened awareness. By practicing mindfulness in photography, you can capture images that are more meaningful, visually engaging, and reflective of the present moment.

To photograph with mindfulness, start by grounding yourself in the present. Take a few deep breaths and bring your attention to the present moment. Let go of any distractions or thoughts that may be pulling you away from the act of photography. By centering yourself, you create a foundation for a more focused and attentive approach.

Paying attention to the details is essential in mindful photography. Take the time to observe the small elements that make up a scene—the textures, patterns, colors, and shapes. By noticing these intricate details, you can create images that are rich in visual interest and depth. Train your eyes to see beyond the obvious and discover the hidden beauty that may go unnoticed by others.

Heightened awareness is a key aspect of mindful photography. Be fully present in your surroundings, attuned to the nuances and subtleties that unfold before your lens. Notice the play of light and shadow, the movement of people or objects, and the ever-changing dynamics of the environment. By being deeply aware, you can anticipate and capture decisive moments that evoke emotions and tell stories.

Let go of any judgments or preconceived notions about what makes a "good" photograph. Instead, approach each scene with a sense of curiosity and open-mindedness. Be receptive to the possibilities and potential in the environment. By releasing expectations, you allow yourself to see things as they truly are and capture images that are authentic and honest.

Embrace the concept of "seeing" rather than just "looking." Train your eyes to truly see beyond the surface and into the heart of a scene. Notice the relationships between different elements, the juxtapositions, and the interplay of colors and shapes. By cultivating this visual awareness, you can compose images that are visually compelling and thought-provoking.

Mindful photography also involves being fully engaged with the process. Slow down and take your time to frame your shot thoughtfully. Consider different angles, perspectives, and compositions. Experiment with different settings and techniques to capture the essence of the scene in the most expressive way. By immersing yourself in the process, you deepen your connection with the subject matter and enhance the quality of your photographs.

Practice gratitude for the opportunity to photograph and for the beauty that surrounds you. Cultivate a sense of appreciation for the present moment and the scenes you encounter. This mindset of gratitude infuses your photography with a positive energy and allows you to capture images that convey a sense of awe and reverence.

Photographing with mindfulness involves paying attention to the details, observing your surroundings with heightened awareness, letting go of judgments, embracing curiosity, and being fully engaged in the process. By practicing mindfulness in photography, you can elevate your images to a new level of depth, meaning, and visual impact. Each photograph becomes a reflection of your connection with the present moment and an invitation for viewers to pause, appreciate, and engage with the image.

Practice Deep Breathing

Taking deep breaths while framing and capturing each shot can bring a sense of calm and focus to your photography practice. The act of breathing deeply can help you center yourself, regulate your emotions, and enhance your overall presence in the moment.

As you prepare to take a shot, take a moment to pause and take a deep breath. Inhale slowly and deeply, filling your lungs with fresh air. As you exhale, release any tension or distractions. This conscious act of breathing allows you to anchor yourself in the present, clearing your mind and bringing a sense of clarity to your photography.

By incorporating deep breaths into your process, you create a natural rhythm and flow that aligns with the act of capturing images. As you breathe in, take in the scene before you, noticing the details, colors, and composition. Let your breath out as you release the shutter, allowing yourself to be fully present and engaged in the moment of capturing the image.

In addition to deep breathing, seeking out peaceful and quiet locations can help cultivate a sense of stillness within yourself. When you are surrounded by tranquility, it becomes easier to find a sense of inner calm and focus. Look for places where you can disconnect from the noise and busyness of everyday life, whether it's a serene natural landscape, a quiet park, or a secluded corner of a bustling city.

In these peaceful environments, take a few moments to absorb the stillness around you. Close your eyes and listen to the gentle sounds of nature or the silence in an urban oasis. Allow yourself to be fully present in this quietude, connecting with the environment on a deeper level. This stillness can create a sense of serenity within you, enabling you to approach your photography with a heightened sense of awareness and mindfulness.

When you find yourself in a peaceful location, take advantage of the opportunity to slow down and truly observe. Notice the subtle details that might go unnoticed in a hurried or chaotic setting. Pay attention to the interplay of light, the textures, and the intricate patterns. By immersing yourself in this environment, you can capture images that convey a sense of tranquility and evoke a feeling of serenity.

Remember that photography is not just about capturing beautiful images; it is also about the experience of being fully present in the moment. The act of taking deep breaths and seeking stillness allows you to connect with your surroundings and yourself on a deeper level. It helps you cultivate a more mindful and introspective approach to your photography, resulting in images that are not only visually striking but also carry a sense of peace and contemplation.

Incorporating deep breaths into your photography practice and seeking out stillness can greatly enhance your ability to be present and focused while capturing each shot. By taking intentional breaths, you bring a sense of calm and clarity to the process. Seeking peaceful and quiet locations allows you to tap into a deeper sense of stillness within yourself. Through these practices, you can cultivate a more mindful and meaningful photography experience, resulting in images that reflect the serenity and beauty of the world around you.

Embrace Imperfection

Capturing moments and scenes as they are, without striving for perfection, is a key aspect of authentic and meaningful photography. It allows you to embrace the imperfections and unique qualities of a moment, resulting in images that convey a sense of honesty, emotion, and genuine connection.

To capture moments as they are, it is important to let go of the pursuit of perfection. Rather than striving for flawless composition or technically impeccable images, focus on the essence and story of the moment. Embrace the imperfections, the unexpected elements, and the raw emotions that unfold before your lens. By accepting and celebrating the imperfections, you create a space for more genuine and relatable photographs.

Be present in the moment and observe without judgment. Instead of trying to manipulate or control the scene, allow it to unfold naturally. By being fully present and attuned to the dynamics of the moment, you can anticipate and capture authentic expressions, gestures, and interactions. This approach ensures that your images are a true reflection of the genuine emotions and experiences of the subjects.

Avoid excessive editing or post-processing that alters the reality of the scene. While post-processing can enhance the visual aesthetics of an image, be mindful of not overly manipulating it to the point where it loses its authenticity. Preserve the integrity of the moment by making minimal adjustments that enhance rather than distort the essence of the scene. By doing so, you maintain the honesty and integrity of the captured moment.

Embrace spontaneity and the element of surprise. Some of the most memorable and impactful images are often the result of serendipitous moments that cannot be planned or staged. Stay open to unexpected opportunities and be ready to capture fleeting moments of beauty or emotion. By embracing spontaneity, you add an element of authenticity and unpredictability to your photographs.

Develop a keen eye for the extraordinary within the ordinary. Train yourself to see the beauty in everyday scenes and moments. Look for the unique perspectives, the fleeting gestures, or the subtle interactions that can transform an ordinary scene into a captivating photograph. By capturing these hidden gems, you reveal the beauty and significance that may be overlooked by others.

Remember that photography is a form of storytelling. Focus on capturing the essence of a moment or scene rather than getting caught up in technical perfection. Pay attention to the emotions, the atmosphere, and the narrative that unfolds before you. By telling the story as it naturally unfolds, you create images that have depth, authenticity, and the power to evoke emotions.

Let go of the pressure to conform to external standards or expectations. Stay true to your own artistic vision and voice. Trust your instincts and intuition when capturing moments. Your unique perspective and personal connection to the subject will shine through in your photographs, making them more impactful and meaningful.

Capturing moments and scenes as they are without striving for perfection allows for the creation of authentic and emotionally resonant photographs. Embrace imperfections, be present, avoid excessive editing, embrace spontaneity, find the extraordinary in the ordinary, focus on storytelling, and trust your instincts. By adopting this approach, you can create images that encapsulate the true essence and beauty of the moments you capture.

Experiment with Light

Exploring different lighting conditions and noticing how they affect your mood and perception is a valuable skill in photography. Light is a powerful tool that can transform a scene, evoke emotions, and enhance the overall impact of an image. By understanding and harnessing the qualities of light, you can create photographs that convey a specific mood or atmosphere.

Start by observing the natural light in different conditions. Notice how the intensity, direction, and color of light change throughout the day and in different weather conditions. Morning and evening light, known as golden hour, often casts a warm and soft glow, creating a romantic and nostalgic feel. Midday light, on the other hand, tends to be harsh and can create strong contrasts and vibrant colors. Cloudy or overcast days can produce diffused light, which is softer and more even, ideal for capturing subtle details and textures.

Experiment with different lighting conditions and observe how they impact your mood and perception of a scene. Pay attention to the way light interacts with the subject, the shadows it creates, and the overall atmosphere it generates. For example, backlighting can create a sense of drama and add a halo effect around the subject. Side lighting can accentuate textures and add depth, while front lighting can provide even illumination but may lack dimensionality. By exploring and understanding these effects, you can choose the most appropriate lighting conditions to convey the desired mood or message in your photographs.

Don't limit yourself to natural light—experiment with artificial lighting as well. Whether it's using a flash, continuous lights, or other lighting modifiers, artificial lighting gives you greater control over the mood and ambiance of a scene. Play with different positions and angles of artificial lights to create dramatic shadows, highlight specific elements, or evoke a particular mood. The ability to manipulate and shape light allows you to add your creative touch and create unique and visually captivating images.

Take the time to connect with the emotions evoked by different lighting conditions. Notice how warm, golden light can create a sense of comfort, nostalgia, or happiness. Conversely, cool or blue light may evoke a feeling of tranquility, mystery, or melancholy. By understanding how lighting affects your own mood and perception, you can use it deliberately to enhance the emotional impact of your photographs.

Pay attention to the interplay between light and shadow. Shadows can add depth, dimension, and visual interest to your images. Experiment with different compositions and angles to emphasize the play of light and shadow. Use shadows to create leading lines, frame the subject, or add a sense of mystery and intrigue.

Remember that the quality of light is just as important as its direction and intensity. Soft, diffused light can create a gentle and serene atmosphere, while harsh light can add drama and create dynamic contrasts. Experiment with different modifiers like reflectors, diffusers, or even translucent materials to manipulate the quality of light and achieve the desired effect.

Developing an understanding of how different lighting conditions affect your mood and perception takes time and practice. Pay attention to the nuances of light in your everyday surroundings, and actively seek out different lighting situations to experiment with. By honing your skills in observing and manipulating light, you can elevate the impact and emotional resonance of your photographs, creating images that truly engage and captivate viewers.

Exploring different lighting conditions and observing how they affect your mood and perception is essential in photography. Take the time to study natural and artificial lighting, experiment with different techniques, and observe the interplay of light and shadow. By understanding the emotional impact of lighting and using it deliberately, you can create photographs that evoke specific moods, tell compelling stories, and leave a lasting impression.

Slow Down

Learning mindfulness and meditation in photography can be achieved by taking your time to compose each shot and avoiding rushing through the process. Mindful photography involves cultivating a deep sense of awareness and presence, allowing you to connect more intimately with the subject matter and create images that reflect your state of mind.

To begin, slow down and resist the urge to rush. Instead of quickly snapping photos, take a deliberate and conscious approach to composing each shot. Give yourself permission to pause, observe, and reflect on the scene before you. By taking your time, you can better appreciate the details, consider different perspectives, and make intentional choices about composition and framing.

Start by exploring the subject from various angles and viewpoints. Move around, get closer or step back, and consider how the different perspectives change the composition and impact the story you want to convey. Experiment with different focal lengths and camera settings to capture the essence of the subject in the most compelling way. By allowing yourself the time to explore and experiment, you can create images that truly resonate with your vision.

While composing each shot, pay attention to the elements within the frame. Notice the relationships between objects, the lines and shapes that guide the viewer's eye, and the balance of positive and negative space. Take a moment to evaluate the overall harmony and visual flow of the composition. By being fully present in this process, you can create images that are visually balanced, engaging, and reflective of your own artistic intention.

Mindful photography also involves being attuned to your emotions and intentions. Notice how you feel as you frame and capture each shot. Are you drawn to certain subjects or scenes? Are you trying to evoke a specific emotion or convey a particular message? By understanding your motivations and emotions, you can align them with your visual choices and create images that reflect your inner state.

As you slow down and immerse yourself in the process of composing each shot, allow yourself to fully engage with the present moment. Let go of distractions, worries, or expectations about the outcome. Instead, focus on the act of photography itself—the interplay of light and shadow, the textures and colors, and the energy of the scene. By bringing a sense of mindful awareness to each moment, you can heighten your connection with the subject and capture its essence more authentically.

Remember that photography is a journey of self-discovery and self-expression. It is an opportunity to express your unique perspective and connect with the world around you. By taking your time and avoiding rushing through the process, you create space for self-reflection, exploration, and creative expression. Photography becomes a meditative practice that allows you to cultivate mindfulness not only in the act of capturing images but also in your approach to life.

Mindfulness and meditation in photography can be achieved by taking your time to compose each shot and avoiding rushing through the process. By slowing down, exploring different perspectives, and paying attention to the elements within the frame, you can create images that reflect your mindful awareness and artistic intention. Embrace photography as a meditative practice that allows you to connect deeply with the present moment, express your unique vision, and cultivate a sense of mindfulness in your creative journey.

Appreciate the Mundane

Mindfulness and meditation can be cultivated by finding beauty in ordinary objects and moments through your camera lens. Mindful photography teaches us to slow down, observe, and appreciate the world around us, allowing us to find beauty in the seemingly mundane and ordinary.

Start by shifting your perspective and noticing the details in everyday life. Instead of seeking grand or extraordinary subjects, focus on the beauty that exists in the ordinary. Look for interesting patterns, textures, colors, and shapes in the objects and scenes that often go unnoticed. By training your eye to see the beauty in the mundane, you develop a greater sense of appreciation and mindfulness.

As you engage with your camera, pay attention to the present moment. Let go of distractions and bring your full awareness to the object or scene you are photographing. Take a moment to connect with the subject and observe it from different angles. By immersing yourself in the act of capturing the image, you cultivate a sense of presence and deepen your connection with the beauty you are capturing.

Take the time to truly see and appreciate the details. Zoom in on the intricacies of a flower petal, the texture of a weathered surface, or the play of light on an everyday object. Notice the interplay of shadows and highlights, the vibrant colors, and the subtleties that make the ordinary extraordinary. By paying attention to these details, you bring a sense of mindfulness to your photography and allow yourself to fully appreciate the beauty in the present moment.

Mindful photography encourages us to let go of judgment and preconceived notions of what is beautiful. Embrace the imperfections, asymmetry, and quirks that make objects and moments unique. See beyond conventional standards of beauty and capture the essence of what resonates with you personally. By finding beauty in the ordinary, you cultivate a deeper sense of acceptance and non-judgment, both in your photography and in life.

Another aspect of mindfulness in photography is slowing down and being patient. Allow the scene to unfold naturally and be receptive to the unexpected. Patience opens up opportunities for capturing fleeting moments, serendipitous interactions, and hidden beauty. By letting go of the need to control or rush, you create space for the magic of the ordinary to reveal itself.

Practice gratitude for the ordinary objects and moments you encounter. Express appreciation for the simple joys and wonders that surround you. Each click of the camera becomes an act of gratitude, capturing and preserving these precious moments. As you develop a habit of gratitude, you cultivate a deeper sense of mindfulness and awareness, both behind the lens and in your daily life.

Remember that photography is not solely about the final image but also about the experience of capturing it. Engaging in mindful photography allows you to approach each shot with a sense of curiosity, openness, and appreciation. It invites you to explore the beauty in the world, connect with the present moment, and express your unique perspective.

Learning mindfulness and meditation through photography involves finding beauty in ordinary objects and moments. By shifting your perspective, paying attention to details, embracing imperfections, being patient, and cultivating gratitude, you develop a mindful approach to photography. Through your camera lens, you can discover and capture the extraordinary within the ordinary, fostering a deeper connection with the present moment and enhancing your overall sense of mindfulness in life.

Practice Patience

Mindfulness and meditation can be fostered by waiting for the right moment to capture a scene or subject, cultivating patience and mindfulness in the process. In photography, patience plays a crucial role in capturing images that convey depth, emotion, and a sense of connection.

When encountering a scene or subject, resist the urge to immediately press the shutter. Instead, take a moment to observe and assess the environment. Pay attention to the elements within the frame, the lighting conditions, and the interactions taking place. By cultivating a patient and mindful approach, you allow yourself to fully immerse in the present moment, opening up the opportunity to capture the essence of the scene.

Patience allows you to wait for the perfect convergence of elements, such as the right lighting, composition, and timing.

By observing and being attuned to the subtle changes happening in the scene, you increase the likelihood of capturing a photograph that truly speaks to the viewer. This patient observation also enables you to anticipate and capture decisive moments that encapsulate the story and emotion within a scene.

During the waiting process, practice mindfulness by anchoring your attention in the present moment. Tune in to your senses—notice the sights, sounds, smells, and sensations around you. Bring your focus to your breath, allowing it to ground you in the present. By immersing yourself fully in the waiting process, you cultivate a sense of stillness and heightened awareness, creating the ideal conditions for capturing impactful photographs.

While waiting, let go of any expectations or desires for a particular outcome. Embrace the uncertainty and trust in the process. This relinquishing of control allows you to remain open and receptive to unexpected opportunities or moments of beauty that may arise. By adopting a mindset of non-attachment, you cultivate a sense of acceptance and flow, which can enhance your ability to capture authentic and spontaneous images.

Use the waiting period as an opportunity for self-reflection and self-awareness. Notice any impatience, restlessness, or wandering thoughts that arise. Acknowledge them without judgment and gently bring your attention back to the present moment. By observing your own mental and emotional states, you deepen your understanding of yourself and develop greater mindfulness in your photography practice.

Remember that patience and waiting do not imply inaction or passivity. While waiting for the right moment, continue to engage with the scene and make subtle adjustments to your composition. Refine your framing, experiment with different angles, or explore alternative perspectives. By remaining actively engaged, you increase the chances of capturing a compelling image when the opportune moment arises.

Celebrate the waiting process itself. Recognize that each moment of waiting is an opportunity for growth, self-discovery, and deepening your connection with the world.

Embrace the patience and mindfulness cultivated during this process and carry it with you beyond photography, enhancing your overall sense of presence and appreciation in daily life.

By cultivating patience, practicing mindfulness, letting go of expectations, and actively engaging with the present moment, you create an environment conducive to capturing images that truly resonate. The waiting process becomes an opportunity for self-reflection, self-awareness, and a deeper connection with the world around you. Embrace the art of waiting and allow it to enrich your photography practice and your journey toward mindfulness.

Notice Patterns

Start by taking the time to observe and appreciate the patterns present in nature. Whether it's the symmetrical petals of a flower, the ripples on a pond, or the intricate patterns on a butterfly's wings, each offers a glimpse into the beauty and order of the natural world. By directing our attention to these patterns, we engage our senses and develop a heightened awareness of the present moment.

Take a closer look at the details within these patterns. Notice the intricacies, textures, and variations that make each pattern unique. Observe how the patterns evolve and change with different lighting conditions or perspectives. By immersing yourself in the observation of patterns, you cultivate a deep sense of presence and mindfulness.

Extend your observation of patterns beyond nature and into your surroundings. Patterns can be found in urban architecture, textiles, or even everyday objects. Pay attention to the lines, shapes, and repetition present in the man-made world. By appreciating these patterns, you develop a sense of connection with your environment and the creative expressions of human ingenuity.

As you observe patterns, practice mindful awareness by bringing your full attention to the present moment. Focus on the intricate details, colors, and textures within the patterns. Notice how your breath flows as you observe, and let go of any distractions or wandering thoughts. By anchoring your attention in the present, you deepen your mindfulness and enhance your ability to fully engage with the patterns before you.

Engage your senses as you explore patterns. Notice the textures under your fingertips, the play of light and shadow on the surface, and the sounds or scents associated with the pattern. By immersing yourself fully in the sensory experience, you deepen your connection with the pattern and develop a richer understanding of its intricacies.

Capture the patterns through your camera lens. Photography can serve as a tool for mindful observation and expression. Frame the patterns in a way that highlights their beauty and uniqueness. Experiment with different angles, perspectives, and focal lengths to capture the essence of the pattern. By capturing these moments, you create visual reminders of the patterns' presence, allowing you to revisit and appreciate them at any time.

Integrate the practice of observing patterns into your daily life. Whether you are taking a walk in nature, waiting in line, or simply sitting in a quiet space, bring your attention to the patterns that surround you. Cultivate a habit of noticing and appreciating the beauty and order within the patterns, no matter how small or seemingly insignificant. By infusing your daily life with this mindful awareness, you create a foundation for a deeper sense of mindfulness and connection with the world.

Mindfulness and meditation can be enhanced by paying attention to patterns in nature or your surroundings and observing their intricacies. By cultivating awareness of patterns, both in nature and the man-made world, we deepen our connection with the present moment and develop a greater appreciation for the beauty and order that surrounds us. Through observation, sensory engagement, photography, and integration into our daily lives, we can embrace the practice of mindfulness and open ourselves to a deeper understanding of ourselves and the world we inhabit.

Practice Mindful Walking

A mindful walk combines the benefits of physical movement, connection with nature, and the meditative practice of photography to create a powerful experience of mindfulness. Begin by setting aside dedicated time for your mindful walk. Choose a location that inspires you—a park, a forest, a beach, or any natural environment that resonates with you. As you embark on your walk, bring your camera along as a tool for deepening your mindfulness and enhancing your connection with the present moment.

As you start walking, bring your attention to your breath and the sensation of your feet touching the ground. Allow your body to move in a relaxed and natural rhythm. Notice how your body feels as it responds to each step, and let any tension or distractions melt away.

Engage your senses fully as you walk. Notice the sights,

sounds, smells, and textures of the environment around you. Be present with each sensory experience, allowing them to anchor you in the present moment. Observe the colors, shapes, and movement of nature. Listen to the rustling of leaves, the chirping of birds, or the sound of water flowing. Feel the warmth of the sun, the coolness of the breeze, or the texture of tree bark. By fully immersing yourself in the sensory experience, you deepen your connection with the present moment and heighten your state of mindfulness.

As you walk, be attentive to the interplay of light and shadow. Notice how the changing light affects the landscape and the mood of the scene. Observe the patterns created by light filtering through the trees or reflecting on water surfaces. Use your camera to capture these moments, allowing the interplay of light and shadow to be preserved and revisited.

Allow your curiosity to guide you as you walk. Let go of any predetermined destination or agenda and allow yourself to be drawn to what captures your attention. Notice the details, both big and small, that intrigue you. It may be a vibrant flower, an interesting rock formation, or a delicate spiderweb. Trust your intuition and follow your photographic instincts as you capture these moments of fascination.

As you pause to take photographs, approach the process with mindfulness and intention. Slow down and take the time to fully observe your subject. Consider different angles, perspectives, and compositions. Be aware of the feelings and emotions that arise as you capture each image. By engaging with your camera in this mindful manner, you deepen your connection with the present moment and create images that reflect your state of mindfulness.

Throughout your mindful walk, stay attuned to your breath and body. Notice any sensations, thoughts, or emotions that arise. Practice non-judgmental awareness, allowing these experiences to come and go without attachment or resistance. Use your camera as a tool for focusing your attention and returning to the present moment whenever you find your mind wandering.

As you conclude your mindful walk, take a moment to reflect on the experience. Acknowledge the moments of mindfulness, connection, and beauty that you encountered. Express gratitude for the opportunity to engage with the present moment and cultivate mindfulness through photography.

By immersing yourself in the sensory experience, observing the interplay of light and shadow, and capturing moments of fascination, you deepen your connection with the world around you and cultivate a state of mindfulness. Embrace the practice of mindful photography as a powerful tool for personal growth, self-expression, and a deeper understanding of yourself and the world.

Play with Perspective

Our experiences can be enhanced by experimenting with different angles and perspectives to see things in a new light. Often, we become accustomed to viewing the world from a fixed perspective, limiting our perception and understanding of the present moment. By consciously exploring alternative angles and perspectives, we open ourselves to fresh insights and a deeper sense of mindfulness.

To begin, approach familiar subjects or scenes with a sense of curiosity and openness. Instead of settling for the default viewpoint, challenge yourself to find alternative angles and perspectives that offer a unique vantage point. Move around the subject, explore different heights, or get close to the ground. By doing so, you break free from habitual patterns of perception and allow yourself to see things in a new light.

Experimenting with different angles and perspectives serves

as a metaphor for how we can approach life off-camera. Just as the physical act of moving around a subject can reveal hidden details, adopting a flexible mindset and willingness to explore can lead to new insights and expanded awareness in our daily lives.

As you explore alternative angles, notice how the scene transforms before your eyes. Different angles can emphasize certain elements, reveal hidden patterns, or create new compositional opportunities. Take the time to observe and appreciate these shifts in perception. Allow yourself to become fully present with each new perspective, opening your mind to fresh interpretations and possibilities.

Mindfulness comes into play as you actively engage with the present moment while experimenting with different angles and perspectives. Pay attention to your breath and the physical sensations in your body as you move and adjust your position. Stay attuned to your surroundings, observing the interplay of light, shadow, colors, and textures. By anchoring your awareness in the present, you cultivate a deeper sense of mindfulness and connection with the act of exploring.

Embrace the concept of "beginner's mind" as you experiment with different angles and perspectives. Approach each new viewpoint with a sense of curiosity and openness, letting go of preconceived notions or judgments. Allow yourself to see the familiar with fresh eyes, as if encountering it for the first time. By adopting this mindset, you foster a spirit of exploration, receptivity, and wonder, deepening your mindfulness in the process.

Remember that experimentation is a process of discovery, and not every angle or perspective will yield a remarkable result. Embrace the journey itself rather than becoming fixated on the outcome. Stay present and attentive to each moment of exploration, regardless of the final image captured. The goal is not perfection, but rather the cultivation of mindfulness and the expansion of your creative and perceptual boundaries.

Extend the practice of experimenting with different angles and perspectives beyond photography. Apply the same mindset to your everyday experiences. Notice how shifting your perspective can alter your perception and understanding of a situation. By intentionally exploring alternative viewpoints, you develop greater empathy, compassion, and open-mindedness in your interactions with others and the world.

Mindfulness and meditation can be deepened by experimenting with different angles and perspectives to see things in a new light. By breaking free from habitual patterns of perception, embracing the beginner's mind, and actively engaging with the present moment, you cultivate a sense of mindfulness and expand your creative and perceptual boundaries. Allow yourself to be guided by curiosity, openness, and a willingness to see the familiar with fresh eyes. Through photography and everyday life, the practice of exploring different angles and perspectives becomes a pathway to deeper self-awareness, expanded consciousness, and a richer experience of the world around you.

Cultivate Gratitude

Gratitude is a powerful practice that cultivates mindfulness, shifts our perspective, and deepens our connection with the present moment. By acknowledging and appreciating the beauty and abundance that surrounds us, we enhance our capacity for mindfulness and open ourselves to a deeper sense of well-being.

Begin by cultivating a mindset of gratitude as you embark on your photography journey. Before even picking up your camera, take a moment to pause and reflect on the privilege of being able to witness and capture the world's wonders. Acknowledge the gift of sight, the ability to perceive and appreciate the colors, textures, and details that unfold before you. Recognize that each moment presents a unique opportunity to connect with the world through your lens.

As you immerse yourself in the act of capturing images, bring awareness to the feelings of gratitude that arise within you. Pay attention to the beauty that surrounds you, whether it's a breathtaking landscape, a delicate flower, or a candid moment of human connection. Pause and express gratitude for each subject, scene, or moment that you encounter. Recognize the privilege of being able to witness and document these fleeting instances of beauty and significance.

Expressing gratitude can be done silently within yourself or through verbal affirmations. Take a moment to mentally or verbally express gratitude for the opportunity to be present in that particular moment and to engage with the world through your photography. You can express gratitude for the light that illuminates your subject, the intricate details that captivate your attention, or the emotions that are evoked by the scene. By actively cultivating gratitude, you infuse your photography practice with mindfulness and a deeper sense of appreciation.

Extend your practice of gratitude beyond the act of capturing images. Take time to reflect on your photographs and express gratitude for the experiences, emotions, and memories they evoke. Whether you're reviewing your images on a computer or holding physical prints in your hands, allow yourself to savor each image and express gratitude for the stories and moments they represent. This act of reflection and appreciation deepens your connection with the present moment and reinforces a state of mindfulness.

Gratitude can also be directed towards the tools and technology that enable you to engage in photography. Whether it's a high-end camera or a simple smartphone, express gratitude for the equipment that allows you to capture and preserve moments of beauty. Recognize the role of technology in expanding your creative possibilities and facilitating your photography practice.

Incorporate gratitude into your daily life beyond photography. Take moments throughout your day to express gratitude for the simple joys, the kindness of others, and the blessings that come your way. By cultivating an attitude of gratitude, you develop a heightened awareness of the abundance and beauty that exist in your experiences. This mindset of gratitude permeates your photography, enriching your capacity for mindfulness and deepening your connection with the world.

Learning mindfulness and meditation can be enhanced by expressing gratitude for the opportunity to capture and appreciate the world around you. By recognizing the privilege of witnessing and documenting moments of beauty, expressing gratitude for the subjects and scenes that unfold before you, and extending gratitude beyond photography into your daily life, you deepen your mindfulness and enhance your connection with the present moment. Embrace the practice of gratitude as a powerful tool for cultivating awareness, appreciation, and a profound sense of well-being in your photography journey and beyond.

Explore Minimalism

Mindfulness and meditation can be deepened by focusing on simplicity and minimalism in your compositions, allowing you to eliminate distractions and cultivate a heightened sense of awareness and presence. Begin by intentionally simplifying your compositions. Instead of trying to capture every element within a scene, focus on identifying the essential components that convey your intended message or evoke a particular emotion. Embrace the philosophy of "less is more" and strive for clarity and simplicity in your compositions. By eliminating unnecessary elements, you create a visual space that encourages a sense of calm and stillness, fostering a deeper connection with the present moment.

One way to achieve simplicity in your compositions is by consciously considering the elements of design, such as lines, shapes, and negative space. Pay attention to the lines and how they guide the viewer's eye. Simplify complex scenes by emphasizing strong lines or finding geometric patterns that bring order and balance. Emphasize shapes that convey meaning or evoke a particular mood. Allow negative space, the empty areas surrounding your subject, to provide breathing room and draw attention to the essential elements. By consciously attending to these design elements, you can create compositions that are visually impactful and conducive to mindfulness.

Mindfulness is also cultivated through the process of eliminating distractions. In a world filled with constant sensory stimulation, learning to quiet the mind and focus on the present moment becomes essential. As you compose your photographs, pay attention to elements that may distract from the intended message or evoke a sense of clutter. Remove unnecessary objects, simplify busy backgrounds, or adjust your perspective to exclude distractions from the frame. By intentionally eliminating distractions, you create a visual space that encourages a deeper sense of mindfulness and allows the viewer to focus on the essential elements of your composition.

Simplicity and minimalism extend beyond the physical aspects of your composition. They also encompass your mindset and approach to photography. Cultivate a mindset of minimalism by letting go of attachments to expectations, desires, or judgments. Approach each moment with an open mind and a willingness to embrace what is present, rather than seeking for what is lacking or wishing for different circumstances. By simplifying your mental landscape, you create space for mindfulness to flourish.

The practice of focusing on simplicity and minimalism in your compositions extends beyond photography and can be applied to various aspects of your life. Embrace the philosophy of minimalism by decluttering your physical space, simplifying your daily routines, and being intentional with your choices. By eliminating excess and focusing on what truly matters, you create an environment that supports mindfulness and cultivates a sense of clarity and purpose.

By intentionally simplifying your compositions, attending to design elements, and eliminating distractions, you create a visual space that encourages mindfulness and a deeper connection with the present moment. Extend the practice of simplicity and minimalism beyond photography into other areas of your life, allowing the principles to guide your mindset and actions. Embrace the power of simplicity as a pathway to mindfulness, clarity, and a greater appreciation for the beauty and essence of each moment.

Capture Emotions

Photography has the unique ability to capture and convey emotions, allowing you to dive deeper into the realm of mindfulness and self-discovery. Learning mindfulness and meditation can be enriched by using your camera as a tool to express and explore your own emotions and those of others.

To begin, take the time to connect with your own emotions before picking up your camera. Tune into your inner world and become aware of the emotions that are present within you. It could be joy, sadness, curiosity, or any other feeling. Allow yourself to fully experience and acknowledge these emotions without judgment. By cultivating this self-awareness, you lay the foundation for using your camera as a means of expression and exploration.

As you embark on your photography journey, pay attention to the emotions that arise within you when observing your surroundings. Notice how certain scenes, colors, or compositions evoke specific emotional responses. Use your camera as a tool to capture these emotions visually. Experiment with different techniques, such as playing with light and shadow, adjusting focus, or capturing fleeting moments of human expression. Allow your camera to become an extension of your emotional landscape, allowing you to externalize and explore the intricacies of your inner world.

In addition to expressing your own emotions, photography can also be a powerful tool for empathetically connecting with the emotions of others. By observing and capturing the emotions expressed by people, animals, or even inanimate objects, you develop a deeper sense of empathy and understanding. Pay attention to the nuances of facial expressions, body language, and the interplay of emotions within a scene. Through your camera lens, seek to capture and convey the genuine emotions experienced by others.

Photography can also serve as a means of exploration and self-discovery. As you venture into different environments and engage with diverse subjects, remain open to the emotions and stories that unfold before you. Allow your camera to be a vehicle for exploring the depths of the human experience. Capture candid moments, unguarded expressions, and the subtle beauty found in everyday life. Through your photographic journey, you may discover new aspects of yourself and gain insights into the interconnectedness of all beings.

Practice mindfulness as you use your camera to express and explore emotions. Be fully present in each moment, immersing yourself in the process of capturing images. Allow yourself to become completely absorbed in the act of framing, adjusting settings, and pressing the shutter button. Pay attention to the details, the interplay of light and shadow, and the emotions that arise within you as you compose each shot. By engaging in the present moment with a sense of focused attention, you deepen your mindfulness and create a space for authentic self-expression.

Extend the practice of using your camera to express and explore emotions beyond photography itself. Reflect on the emotions captured in your images, journaling or engaging in creative activities to further delve into their significance. Share your photographs with others, inviting them to connect with the emotions you have captured and fostering meaningful conversations. By actively engaging with the emotions expressed in your images, you invite a deeper understanding of yourself and others.

Mindfulness and meditation can be deepened by using your camera to express and explore emotions, both within yourself and in others. By connecting with your own emotions, using your camera to capture and convey feelings, and engaging empathetically with the emotions of others, you create a pathway for self-discovery, empathy, and a deeper connection with the present moment. Embrace photography as a means of expressing your inner world and as a tool for understanding the rich tapestry of human emotions. Allow your camera to be a vehicle for mindfulness and self-expression, inviting you to explore the depths of your own emotions and connect with the shared emotional experiences of others.

Find Balance

Balance is a fundamental principle in photography, and it extends beyond mere compositional techniques. It involves finding a harmonious relationship between the subject and its surroundings, creating a visual equilibrium that evokes a sense of calm and mindfulness.

To begin, pay attention to the relationship between the subject and the background when composing your images. Avoid situations where the subject appears overwhelmed or lost in a busy or distracting background. Instead, strive for balance by ensuring that the subject stands out while still maintaining a sense of harmony with its environment. Experiment with different angles, perspectives, and focal lengths to find the ideal balance that captures the essence of your subject while creating a visually appealing composition.

One way to achieve balance is by using the rule of thirds.

Imagine dividing the frame into a grid of nine equal sections by overlaying two horizontal and two vertical lines. Position the subject or the key elements of interest along these lines or at their intersections. This technique helps create a visually balanced composition and guides the viewer's eye through the image in a pleasing way. Remember that balance doesn't necessarily mean placing the subject in the center of the frame; it's about finding a dynamic equilibrium that engages the viewer's attention.

In addition to the subject-background relationship, consider the visual elements within the frame and their distribution. Aim for symmetry or asymmetrical balance, depending on the mood and intention of your photograph. Symmetry refers to a composition where the elements are evenly balanced on either side of an axis. It can create a sense of stability and order. On the other hand, asymmetrical balance involves placing elements of varying size, shape, or weight in a way that creates a harmonious composition. It can evoke a dynamic and visually interesting image. Experiment with both approaches and trust your intuition to find the balance that resonates with your vision.

Seeking balance in your photographs goes beyond the technical aspects of composition. It also requires cultivating a balanced state of mind. As you approach your photography practice, strive for a sense of inner equilibrium and presence. Be mindful of your thoughts, emotions, and physical sensations. Allow yourself to be fully present in the act of capturing images, letting go of distractions and external pressures. By finding inner balance, you create a receptive state of mind that allows you to notice and capture the visual balance in your surroundings.

Incorporate the practice of seeking balance into your daily life beyond photography. Notice the delicate interplay between various elements, whether it's in nature, architecture, or human interactions. Cultivate an appreciation for the balance that exists in the world around you and bring that awareness into your photography. The act of seeking balance in your compositions becomes a metaphor for seeking balance in life, fostering a sense of mindfulness, harmony, and well-being.

Mindfulness can be deepened by seeking balance between the subject and the background in your compositions. By paying attention to the relationship between the elements within the frame, using techniques like the rule of thirds, and exploring both symmetrical and asymmetrical balance, you create visually harmonious images that reflect a sense of equilibrium. This pursuit of balance extends beyond technical considerations and involves cultivating a balanced state of mind and appreciating balance in the world around you. Embrace the practice of seeking balance as a pathway to mindfulness, visual harmony, and a deeper connection with the present moment.

Practice
Self-Reflection

Using your photography as a tool for self-reflection and personal growth can enhance mindfulness, allowing you to delve deeper into your inner world and cultivate a greater sense of self-awareness.

Begin by approaching your photography practice with a mindset of curiosity and introspection. Rather than solely focusing on capturing aesthetically pleasing images, view your camera as a means of self-expression and exploration. Use your camera as a mirror to reflect upon your thoughts, emotions, and experiences. By bringing mindfulness into your photography, you can tap into a rich source of self-discovery.

As you engage in the process of capturing images, pay attention to your intentions and motivations. Ask yourself why you are drawn to certain subjects, themes, or compositions. Notice the emotions that arise within you when photographing different scenes. Are you drawn to vibrant colors, serene landscapes, or candid human moments? By becoming aware of your inclinations, preferences, and emotional responses, you gain insights into your own inner landscape.

Photography can also serve as a medium for exploring your emotions and expressing your authentic self. Use your camera to capture moments that resonate with you on an emotional level. Seek out subjects or scenes that evoke specific feelings or memories. Experiment with different techniques, such as long exposures or intentional blur, to convey the mood or atmosphere that aligns with your internal state. Allow your photographs to become a visual diary, reflecting your emotions and experiences at different moments in time.

Practice self-reflection by regularly reviewing and analyzing your photographs. Take the time to examine your images with a curious and open mind. Notice the patterns, themes, and recurring motifs that emerge. Reflect upon the emotions and stories that your photographs convey. Consider how your images relate to your personal journey, values, and aspirations. This process of introspection and self-reflection can deepen your understanding of yourself and promote personal growth.

Incorporate mindfulness into your editing process as well. Approach post-processing with a sense of present-moment awareness. Pay attention to the choices you make in adjusting colors, contrast, and composition. Notice how each adjustment affects the mood and message of the image. As you edit, strive for authenticity and congruence between your inner vision and the final result. The process of editing becomes an opportunity for mindful decision-making and self-expression.

Extend the practice of using photography for self-reflection beyond the act of capturing and editing images. Journal about your experiences and observations during your photography outings. Reflect on the lessons and insights you have gained through your photography practice. Engage in conversations with fellow photographers or share your work with trusted friends, inviting their perspectives and interpretations. Embrace the feedback and insights that others offer, as they can deepen your self-awareness and provide new perspectives.

Mindfulness can be enriched by using your photography as a tool for self-reflection and personal growth. By approaching your photography practice with curiosity and introspection, exploring your emotions, and engaging in self-reflection during the process of capturing and editing images, you can deepen your self-awareness and gain valuable insights into your own inner world. Embrace photography as a medium for self-expression, exploration, and personal growth, allowing it to become a powerful tool for mindfulness and self-discovery. Through your photography, embark on a journey of self-reflection and use the images you create as mirrors to understand and embrace your own unique perspectives, emotions, and experiences.

Create a
Visual Diary

Mindfulness can be enriched by documenting your thoughts, experiences, and emotions through a series of photographs, creating a visual diary that serves as a powerful tool for self-reflection and deepening your mindfulness practice.

Begin by setting an intention to use your camera as a means of capturing moments and experiences that hold significance for you. Treat your photography practice as a form of journaling, using images to tell stories and convey your inner world. As you embark on this journey, allow yourself to be fully present in each moment, immersing yourself in the act of capturing images with a sense of mindful awareness.

Use your camera to document not only the external world but also your internal landscape. Pay attention to your thoughts, emotions, and sensations as you frame and capture each photograph. Notice how certain scenes or subjects elicit specific reactions within you. Document moments that evoke joy, curiosity, contemplation, or any other emotions that arise. Allow your photographs to serve as a mirror, reflecting your inner experiences and capturing the essence of your thoughts and emotions.

Create a regular practice of reviewing and reflecting upon your photographic diary. Set aside dedicated time to immerse yourself in the images you have captured. Notice the stories they tell and the emotions they evoke. Reflect upon the moments and experiences they represent. Consider how the images relate to your personal journey, values, and aspirations. This process of self-reflection and contemplation deepens your mindfulness and helps you gain a greater understanding of yourself.

Alongside your photographs, incorporate written reflections and thoughts to accompany your visual diary. Write about the experiences that led you to capture particular images, the emotions they evoke, and the insights you have gained through the process. Use words to further explore and articulate your thoughts and feelings, allowing your written reflections to complement and enhance the visual narrative.

As you document your thoughts, experiences, and emotions through your photographic diary, notice any patterns or themes that emerge. Pay attention to the recurring motifs or subjects that draw your attention. Observe how your interests, perspectives, and emotions evolve over time. Use these observations to deepen your self-awareness, gain insights into your own growth and development, and foster personal transformation.

Share your photographic diary with trusted friends or participate in supportive photography communities. Invite others to engage with your visual diary and provide their perspectives and interpretations. Embrace the feedback and insights that others offer, as they can deepen your self-reflection and provide new perspectives. Engage in conversations that arise from your shared experiences, allowing them to further enrich your mindfulness practice.

In addition to documenting your own thoughts and emotions, use your photography to observe and capture the world around you with a heightened sense of awareness. Practice mindful observation by immersing yourself in the present moment, noticing the details, textures, and colors of your surroundings. Use your camera to capture the beauty in ordinary objects and everyday moments, recognizing the inherent value and significance in each.

Documenting your thoughts, experiences, and emotions through a series of photographs to create a visual diary can enhance mindfulness. By treating your photography practice as a form of journaling, reflecting upon your images, and incorporating written reflections, you engage in a process of self-reflection and self-discovery. Use your photographic diary to explore your internal landscape, notice patterns and themes, and deepen your self-awareness. Share your visual diary with others to foster meaningful conversations and gain new perspectives. Through the act of documenting and reflecting upon your thoughts and experiences, you cultivate mindfulness and create a powerful tool for personal growth and transformation.

Experiment with Long Exposures

Mindfulness and meditation can be enhanced by incorporating long exposure techniques into your photography practice, allowing you to create ethereal and meditative images that evoke a sense of calm, stillness, and contemplation.

Long exposure photography involves using longer shutter speeds to capture the movement of subjects over an extended period. By extending the exposure time, you can create beautiful effects such as silky smooth water, streaking clouds, and blurred motion. These techniques not only produce visually captivating images but also provide an opportunity to cultivate mindfulness and deepen your meditation practice.

To begin, find a suitable subject that lends itself well to long exposure photography. Consider natural elements like flowing water, crashing waves, or swaying trees. Urban environments with bustling crowds or moving traffic can also be compelling subjects. Choose a scene that resonates with you and invites a sense of serenity and contemplation.

Set up your camera on a sturdy tripod to ensure stability during the long exposure. Use a neutral density (ND) filter to reduce the amount of light entering the lens, allowing for longer shutter speeds even in bright conditions. This enables you to capture the desired motion effect without overexposing the image.

Once your camera is set up, take a moment to connect with the present moment and engage in mindful awareness. Bring your attention to the scene before you, observing the movement and flow of the subject. Notice the subtle details, textures, and colors that surround you. Be fully present and immersed in the present moment.

When you are ready, choose an appropriate shutter speed that will capture the desired motion effect. Experiment with different exposure times to achieve the desired ethereal and meditative look. It may take some trial and error to find the perfect balance between motion blur and clarity.

As you engage in the process of capturing long exposure images, bring your attention to the movement and flow of the subject. Observe the continuous changes unfolding before you. Notice how the subject transforms over time, blurring and merging into a fluid and interconnected whole. Allow yourself to become absorbed in this visual meditation, letting go of distractions and entering a state of deep presence.

While the camera is capturing the long exposure, take the opportunity to immerse yourself in the stillness and silence of the moment. Pay attention to your breath, using it as an anchor to the present. Allow the experience to unfold with a sense of mindful awareness, embracing the beauty and tranquility that surrounds you.

After capturing the image, take the time to review and reflect upon the results. Notice the patterns, textures, and colors that emerge from the long exposure. Reflect upon the emotions and sensations that the image evokes within you. Consider how the ethereal and meditative qualities of the photograph align with your own inner state and experiences.

Incorporate the practice of long exposure photography into your regular mindfulness and meditation routine. Take intentional outings specifically dedicated to capturing long exposure images. Engage in these photography sessions with a sense of curiosity, exploration, and mindful awareness. Allow yourself to be fully present and open to the unexpected beauty that arises through the long exposure process.

Mindfulness and meditation can be deepened by incorporating long exposure techniques into your photography practice. By using longer shutter speeds to capture the movement of subjects, you create ethereal and meditative images that evoke a sense of calm and contemplation. As you engage in the process of capturing long exposure photographs, cultivate mindfulness and deepen your meditation practice by connecting with the present moment, observing the movement and flow of the subject, and immersing yourself in the stillness and silence of the experience. Embrace the opportunity to reflect upon the results, noticing the patterns and emotions that emerge.

Engage Your Senses

Paying attention to the textures, colors, sounds, and smells around you as you engage in the process of photography can deepen mindfulness. By honing your senses and immersing yourself fully in the present moment, you can cultivate a heightened awareness and enhance your mindfulness practice.

When you embark on a photography session, take a moment to ground yourself and bring your attention to the present. Notice the textures that surround you—the roughness of tree bark, the smoothness of water, or the delicate petals of a flower. As you compose your shot, run your fingers over the surfaces, feeling the tactile sensations and connecting with the physical world.

Direct your attention to the colors that fill your frame. Observe the hues, tones, and shades that catch your eye. Allow yourself to be fully present with the richness and variety of colors that exist in the scene. Notice how different colors evoke different emotions or moods. Stay attuned to the interplay of light and color, and how they transform the atmosphere of the moment.

As you engage in photography, pay attention to the sounds that surround you. Close your eyes for a moment and listen to the symphony of nature or the urban environment. Hear the rustling of leaves, the gentle flow of a stream, or the distant hum of city life. Allow the sounds to draw you into the present moment and deepen your connection to the scene you are capturing.

Engage your sense of smell as you photograph. Notice the scents that waft through the air—the fragrance of blooming flowers, the crispness of the outdoors, or the aroma of food being prepared nearby. Take a deep breath and let the scents transport you to the present, heightening your sensory experience and anchoring you in the moment.

As you pay attention to these sensory details, let go of any judgments or preconceived notions. Embrace a mindset of curiosity and openness, allowing yourself to fully immerse in the present experience. Be receptive to the sensory information that surrounds you, without labeling or analyzing it. Simply observe and experience each sensation as it unfolds.

As you engage your senses, practice mindful awareness of the present moment. Allow the textures, colors, sounds, and smells to become anchors for your attention, grounding you in the here and now. Let go of past and future concerns, and be fully present with what is unfolding before you. By training your attention on the sensory experience of the present, you cultivate a state of mindfulness.

Extend this practice of sensory awareness beyond photography outings and incorporate it into your daily life. Take moments throughout the day to notice the textures, colors, sounds, and smells that surround you. Whether you are indoors or outdoors, engage your senses and bring a mindful awareness to the present moment. By integrating this practice into your daily routine, you strengthen your ability to be present and cultivate a deeper sense of mindfulness.

Learning mindfulness and meditation can be enriched by

paying attention to the textures, colors, sounds, and smells around you as you engage in photography. By immersing yourself fully in the sensory experience of the present moment, you deepen your connection to the world and enhance your mindfulness practice. Embrace the textures, observe the colors, listen to the sounds, and inhale the scents that unfold around you. Allow these sensory experiences to anchor you in the present, cultivating a heightened state of awareness and deepening your mindfulness practice both in photography and in life.

Create
Still Lifes

Mindfulness and meditation can be enhanced by arranging objects mindfully and photographing them to evoke a sense of calm and contemplation. By engaging in the process of mindful arrangement and capturing the beauty of these arrangements through photography, you can deepen your mindfulness practice and create visual reminders of tranquility and balance.

Begin by selecting a few objects that resonate with you and bring a sense of peace or joy. These objects can be natural elements such as stones, flowers, or leaves, or man-made items like candles, shells, or art pieces. Choose objects that have significance to you or that embody qualities you wish to cultivate, such as serenity, harmony, or mindfulness.

Create a dedicated space where you can arrange the objects mindfully. Clear a small area and place a clean and uncluttered backdrop, such as a plain tablecloth or a piece of fabric. This will provide a simple and neutral background that allows the objects to take center stage.

As you arrange the objects, do so with intention and mindfulness. Pay attention to the placement, orientation, and relationship between the objects. Take your time to find a harmonious arrangement that brings a sense of balance and tranquility. Be present with each movement, noticing the textures, shapes, and colors of the objects as you handle them.

As you arrange the objects, let go of any expectations or judgments. Instead, allow yourself to fully immerse in the process, observing and adjusting until you feel a sense of alignment and coherence. Use your intuition and creativity to guide the arrangement, letting it unfold naturally.

Once you have created the arrangement, take a moment to appreciate the beauty and harmony that you have created. Allow yourself to be fully present with the arrangement, taking in the details and experiencing the serenity it evokes. Engage your senses by observing the textures, colors, and shapes of the objects, and notice how they interact with one another.

Now, it's time to capture the arrangement through photography. Set up your camera and tripod, ensuring stability and clarity in your images. Choose a perspective and framing that best highlights the arrangement and the qualities you wish to convey. Experiment with different angles and compositions to find the one that resonates with your vision.

As you photograph the arrangement, maintain a sense of mindfulness and presence. Pay attention to the light, shadows, and reflections that interact with the objects. Observe how the camera lens captures the textures, colors, and details. Be patient and take your time to find the right moment and exposure settings that best capture the essence of the arrangement.

After capturing the images, take a moment to review and reflect upon them. Observe the composition, the interplay of colors and shapes, and the overall mood they convey. Notice how the images evoke a sense of calm, balance, and contemplation. Reflect on the intention behind the arrangement and the qualities you aimed to evoke. Allow the images to serve as reminders of mindfulness and the beauty of simplicity.

As you engage in this practice, explore different arrangements and experiment with various objects and themes. Allow your creativity to flow and follow your intuition as you arrange and photograph. Embrace this process as a form of meditation, where you can immerse yourself in the present moment and express your inner state through the visual medium.

Learning mindfulness and meditation can be deepened by arranging objects mindfully and photographing them to evoke a sense of calm and contemplation. By engaging in this practice, you cultivate a heightened sense of awareness and presence, both during the arrangement process and through capturing the beauty of the arrangements in photographs. This practice allows you to create visual reminders of tranquility and balance, which can serve as anchors for mindfulness in your daily life. Embrace the opportunity to explore your creativity, express your inner state, and cultivate a sense of harmony and serenity

Notice Transitions

Capturing moments of transition and change through photography, symbolizing the impermanence of life can be very meditative. By consciously seeking out and photographing these moments, you can cultivate a deeper understanding of impermanence and embrace the present moment with greater appreciation and mindfulness.

Transition and change are inherent aspects of life. They manifest in various forms, such as the shifting of seasons, the ebb and flow of tides, the growth and decay of plants, and the passage of time. These moments hold profound lessons about the impermanence and interconnectedness of all things.

To capture moments of transition and change, be attuned to the subtle shifts and transformations happening around you. Observe the changing colors of the leaves in autumn, the blossoming of flowers in spring, or the melting snow in winter.

Pay attention to the cycles of nature and the markers of time that indicate the passing of seasons.

When you notice a moment of transition or change, pause and bring your attention to the present. Take a few deep breaths to center yourself and cultivate mindfulness. Observe the scene before you, noting the details and nuances that reflect the impermanence of the moment. Engage your senses to fully experience the beauty and significance of the transition unfolding.

As you compose your shot, consider how you can convey the sense of impermanence through your photography. Seek out elements that represent both the passing and emerging stages of the transition. Look for juxtapositions and contrasts that highlight the fleeting nature of the moment. Experiment with different angles, perspectives, and framing to capture the essence of the transition.

Pay attention to the interplay of light and shadow, as they can accentuate the mood and emphasize the transient nature of the scene. Notice how the changing light affects the colors, textures, and overall atmosphere of the moment. Use these elements to evoke a sense of impermanence and capture the fleeting beauty of the transition.

As you click the shutter, maintain a sense of presence and mindfulness. Be fully engaged in the process, embracing the impermanence of the moment as it is preserved in the photograph. Allow yourself to let go of attachments to the outcome and surrender to the flow of change. Embrace the opportunity to capture the beauty and significance of the moment, knowing that it will never be the same again.

After capturing the image, take the time to reflect upon it. Observe the elements that symbolize transition and change. Reflect on the impermanence they represent and the lessons they hold. Consider how the photograph serves as a reminder of the fleeting nature of life and the importance of embracing each moment with mindfulness and appreciation.

Integrate this practice of capturing moments of transition and change into your daily life. Cultivate an awareness of the impermanence unfolding around you and seek out opportunities to document these moments through photography. Embrace the lessons they offer and allow them to deepen your understanding of impermanence and enhance your mindfulness practice.

Mindfulness and meditation can be deepened by capturing moments of transition and change through photography. By intentionally seeking out these moments and symbolizing the impermanence of life, you cultivate a deeper awareness and appreciation for the present moment. Embrace the opportunity to observe and capture the subtle shifts and transformations happening around you. Use photography as a means to convey the essence of impermanence and embrace the fleeting beauty of the transitions unfolding. Allow these photographs to serve as reminders of the preciousness of each moment and the importance of cultivating mindfulness and appreciation in all aspects of life.

Focus on Details

Zooming in on small details through photography, cultivating a sense of concentration and attention to the present moment can be a mindful practice. By intentionally focusing on the intricate and often overlooked elements of the world around us, we can develop a deep sense of presence and sharpen our ability to observe and appreciate the beauty in the present moment.

When engaging in photography, take the time to observe your surroundings and identify the small details that catch your eye. These details can be found in nature, such as the delicate patterns on a flower petal, the intricate texture of a tree bark, or the glistening dewdrops on a blade of grass. They can also be found in everyday objects, like the texture of fabric, the grains on a wooden surface, or the play of light on a reflective surface.

Once you have identified a detail that captivates you, bring your attention fully to it. Zoom in with your camera or get closer physically to the subject, allowing yourself to immerse in its intricacies. Notice the lines, shapes, colors, and textures that make up the detail. Observe how light interacts with the surface, creating highlights and shadows that accentuate its unique qualities.

As you zoom in on the small detail, let go of any distractions or preoccupations. Direct your full attention to the present moment, engaging your senses and observing the detail with openness and curiosity. Notice the subtle nuances and variations within the detail, and allow yourself to become absorbed in its beauty.

While focusing on the small detail, practice cultivating a sense of concentration and attention. Allow yourself to enter a state of flow, where your mind becomes fully engaged in the observation of the detail. Release any judgments or thoughts that arise, and simply be present with the experience of observing and capturing the detail through your lens.

Pay attention to your breath as you immerse in the observation. Take slow, deep breaths to anchor yourself in the present moment. Use the rhythm of your breath as a reminder to stay centered and focused. This conscious breathing helps calm the mind, enhance concentration, and deepen your connection to the detail you are photographing.

As you capture the detail through photography, experiment with different compositions and angles. Explore various perspectives that highlight the uniqueness and beauty of the detail. Play with depth of field to create a sense of focus and depth in the image. Allow your creativity to flow and trust your intuition as you compose the shot.

After capturing the image, take a moment to reflect and appreciate the small detail you have focused on. Observe the photograph and notice how it reflects the essence and intricacy of the detail. Allow yourself to be fully present with the image, appreciating the beauty and significance of the small detail you have captured.

Integrate this practice of zooming in on small details into your daily life. Develop the habit of noticing and appreciating the small intricacies that surround you, whether you have your camera with you or not. Cultivate a sense of concentration and attention to the present by regularly engaging in this practice of observing and capturing the small details that often go unnoticed.

Learning mindfulness and meditation can be deepened by zooming in on small details through photography. By intentionally focusing on these details and immersing ourselves in their intricacies, we develop a sense of concentration and attention to the present moment. Embrace the opportunity to observe and appreciate the beauty in the small details of the world around you. Allow photography to serve as a tool for cultivating mindfulness and sharpening your ability to observe and appreciate the present moment.

Document Gratitude

Mindfulness and meditation can be enriched by taking pictures of things you are grateful for and creating a gratitude photo journal. By intentionally focusing on the positive aspects of life and capturing them through photography, you can cultivate a deeper sense of gratitude, enhance your mindfulness practice, and create a visual record of the things that bring you joy and appreciation.

To begin, take a moment each day to reflect on the things you are grateful for. These can be simple pleasures, meaningful experiences, or the presence of loved ones. Allow yourself to fully immerse in the feelings of gratitude and appreciation for these aspects of your life.

Once you have identified something you are grateful for, grab your camera and capture it through photography. It can be a physical object, a beautiful view, a moment of connection, or anything else that evokes a sense of gratitude within you. Seek out the qualities that make it special and unique.

As you frame and compose your shot, be mindful of your intention to express gratitude. Pay attention to the details and elements that make the subject of your photograph significant to you. Consider the lighting, colors, textures, and overall atmosphere that can enhance the representation of gratitude in your image.

When you are ready, press the shutter and capture the photograph. Allow yourself to fully experience the moment of capturing something you are grateful for. Be present with the process, acknowledging the gratitude in your heart as you document it through photography.

After capturing the image, take a few moments to reflect on the feelings and thoughts it evokes. Observe the details, composition, and overall mood of the photograph. Allow yourself to be fully present with the gratitude it represents, appreciating the beauty and significance of the moment you have captured.

Create a gratitude photo journal to compile and document your photographs of gratitude. This can be a physical album, a digital collection, or an online platform. As you add new photographs, take the time to revisit the images you have captured previously. Allow them to serve as reminders of the things that bring you joy, appreciation, and gratitude.

Regularly engage with your gratitude photo journal as part of your mindfulness and meditation practice. Set aside time to review the photographs, immersing yourself in the positive emotions they evoke. Use the visual reminders to anchor yourself in the present moment and cultivate a deep sense of gratitude and appreciation for the blessings in your life.

As you explore this practice, you may also choose to share your gratitude photographs with others. Allow them to inspire and uplift those around you, spreading the positive energy of gratitude. Encourage others to find their own moments of gratitude and capture them through photography, fostering a collective sense of appreciation and mindfulness.

Mindfulness and meditation can be enhanced by taking pictures of things you are grateful for and creating a gratitude photo journal. By intentionally focusing on the positive aspects of life and capturing them through photography, you cultivate a deeper sense of gratitude, enhance your mindfulness practice, and create a visual record of joy and appreciation. Embrace the opportunity to reflect on and document the things that bring you gratitude, and allow your gratitude photo journal to serve as a powerful reminder of the blessings in your life.

Reflect on Light and Shadow

Light and shadow are powerful elements that can evoke different moods, highlight textures, and create a sense of depth and dimension in an image. By consciously paying attention to their dynamics and capturing their interplay, you can develop a heightened sense of awareness, enhance your mindfulness practice, and create visually compelling photographs.

Start by finding a scene or subject that catches your eye and allows for interesting play of light and shadow. It could be a landscape, a still life arrangement, or even a portrait. Take a moment to observe the light sources and the direction from which they illuminate the scene. Notice the quality of light—whether it is soft and diffused, or harsh and direct—and how it interacts with the surrounding environment.

As you compose your shot, consider how you can incorporate

both light and shadow to create visual interest and depth. Look for areas where the light falls on your subject, creating highlights and revealing details. Similarly, observe the shadow areas and how they contribute to the overall mood and atmosphere of the scene. Experiment with different angles and perspectives to capture the interplay between light and shadow from various vantage points.

While engaging with the scene, bring your attention fully to the present moment. Notice the subtle changes in light and shadow as they shift and transform with time. Be mindful of how they affect your perception of the subject and the overall mood of the scene. Allow yourself to become fully immersed in the observation of light and shadow, letting go of distractions and preoccupations.

As you click the shutter, be attentive to your breath. Take slow, deep breaths to anchor yourself in the present moment and enhance your focus. Use the rhythm of your breath as a reminder to stay present and attuned to the interplay between light and shadow. Allow yourself to enter a state of flow, where your mind becomes fully absorbed in the observation and capture of this dynamic interaction.

After capturing the image, take a moment to review and reflect upon it. Observe how the interplay of light and shadow has influenced the composition, mood, and visual impact of the photograph. Pay attention to the way light and shadow have shaped the subject, emphasizing certain aspects and creating a sense of depth. Allow yourself to appreciate the beauty and significance of their interplay in the captured moment.

Integrate this practice of observing and capturing the interplay of light and shadow into your daily life. Develop the habit of noticing how light and shadow interact in your surroundings, even when you don't have your camera with you. Cultivate a heightened awareness of their dynamics and the impact they have on your perception and mood.

Learning mindfulness and meditation can be enhanced by observing how light and shadow interact and capturing their interplay through photography. By consciously engaging with the dynamics of light and shadow, you develop a heightened sense of awareness, enhance your mindfulness practice, and create visually compelling images. Embrace the opportunity to observe and capture the interplay between light and shadow in your photographs, and allow their beauty and significance to deepen your connection to the present moment.

Meditative Landscapes

Engaging with nature through photography allows us to immerse ourselves in the present moment, appreciate the beauty around us, and cultivate a deep sense of calm and connectedness. By intentionally seeking out and capturing serene landscapes, we can enhance our mindfulness practice and create images that evoke a sense of tranquility.

Start by exploring natural environments that resonate with you, such as forests, mountains, beaches, or meadows. Seek out locations that offer a sense of peace and serenity, where you can connect with the stillness and beauty of the natural world. Be open to discovering new places that instill a sense of tranquility within you.

As you arrive at your chosen landscape, take a few moments to simply be present and observe your surroundings. Pay attention to the colors, shapes, textures, and sounds that greet you. Take note of the elements that evoke a feeling of calmness, whether it's the gentle rustling of leaves, the soft hues of a sunset, or the vast expanse of a serene lake.

When you're ready to capture the landscape through photography, approach it with a sense of mindfulness. Be fully present with the scene, allowing yourself to connect deeply with its energy and atmosphere. Take your time to compose the shot, considering the elements that evoke a sense of tranquility. Experiment with different angles, perspectives, and focal points to convey the serenity of the landscape.

As you engage with the landscape, let go of any distractions or preoccupations. Focus your attention solely on the present moment and the beauty before you. Take slow, deep breaths to anchor yourself in the experience, allowing each inhalation and exhalation to deepen your connection with the landscape.

Notice the subtle details that contribute to the overall serenity of the scene. Pay attention to the interplay of light and shadows, the softness of the breeze, and the delicate balance of elements in the landscape. Use your camera as a tool to capture and preserve these moments of tranquility, allowing them to serve as reminders of the peace and calm you experienced.

After capturing the image, take a moment to review it and reflect on the feelings and emotions it evokes. Observe the composition, colors, and overall mood of the photograph. Allow yourself to be fully present with the image, appreciating the tranquility it represents and the connection you felt with the landscape.

Integrate this practice of photographing serene landscapes into your regular mindfulness and meditation routine. Set aside dedicated time to seek out peaceful locations and immerse yourself in their beauty. Use your camera as a means to deepen your connection with nature and to capture the serenity and peace that resonates within you.

Additionally, surround yourself with these serene images in your daily life. Display them in your home, use them as screensavers or wallpapers, or create a physical or digital album dedicated to your tranquil landscape photographs.

Allow these images to serve as visual reminders of the peace and tranquility you have experienced, bringing a sense of calm into your everyday environment.

Learning mindfulness and meditation can be facilitated by photographing serene landscapes that inspire a sense of tranquility and peace. By intentionally seeking out and capturing these landscapes, we deepen our connection with nature, cultivate a sense of calm, and create images that evoke serenity. Embrace the opportunity to immerse yourself in the beauty of serene landscapes through photography and allow them to enhance your mindfulness practice.

Practice Non-Judgment

Photography, as a form of creative expression, is deeply personal and subjective. By letting go of self-criticism and comparison, you can cultivate a mindset of non-judgment, foster self-acceptance, and create photographs that authentically reflect your unique perspective and experiences.

First and foremost, recognize that every photograph you capture is a reflection of your individual vision and interpretation. Embrace the understanding that there is no right or wrong when it comes to artistic expression. Each image is an expression of your personal creativity, emotions, and experiences in that particular moment.

Instead of seeking external validation or comparison, focus on cultivating an internal sense of satisfaction and contentment with your work. Embrace the process of creating photographs as a means of self-discovery and exploration. Allow yourself the freedom to experiment, take risks, and learn from each experience, rather than striving for perfection or comparing yourself to others.

Practice mindfulness by observing your thoughts and emotions as they arise while reviewing your photographs. Notice any tendencies to judge or criticize your work. Instead of getting caught up in these judgments, redirect your attention to the present moment and the process of creating. Remind yourself that your photographs are an expression of your unique perspective, and honor them as a reflection of your personal journey.

Develop a sense of curiosity and openness towards your own work. Rather than focusing solely on the final result, pay attention to the process and the emotions it evokes within you. Be receptive to the lessons and insights that each photograph offers, whether it's technical growth, emotional expression, or a new way of seeing the world. Allow your photographs to be a source of self-reflection and self-discovery.

Cultivate self-compassion by acknowledging that photography, like any skill, is a continuous learning process. Embrace the understanding that growth and improvement come with time and practice. Celebrate the small victories and milestones along your creative journey, appreciating the progress you make rather than comparing yourself to others.

Practice gratitude for the ability to capture and express yourself through photography. Embrace the joy and fulfillment that come from the act of creation itself, regardless of external validation. Each photograph is a testament to your unique perspective and experiences, and by focusing on gratitude, you shift your attention to the positive aspects of your creative practice.

Seek inspiration from others' work without comparing yourself to them. Explore the photographs of fellow photographers, artists, and masters of the craft with an open mind and a desire to learn. Appreciate their unique styles, techniques, and perspectives, allowing them to inspire and inform your own work. Remember, however, that your journey as a photographer is distinct, and your path is shaped by your own experiences and vision.

Mindfulness and meditation can be supported by avoiding judgment of your own photographs and refraining from comparing them to others'. Embrace the understanding that photography is a personal form of expression, and each photograph is a reflection of your unique perspective and experiences. Cultivate self-acceptance, practice gratitude, and focus on the process of creation rather than seeking external validation. Allow photography to be a means of self-discovery, growth, and joy, appreciating the beauty of your own unique vision.

Practice Mindful Sharing

By approaching the act of sharing with consciousness and awareness, you can enhance your mindfulness practice, foster meaningful connections, and contribute to the well-being of others through your creative expression.

Before sharing your photographs, take a moment to reflect on your intentions. Ask yourself why you want to share your work and what message or feeling you wish to convey. Cultivate an intention of inspiring and uplifting others, rather than seeking validation or attention. Shift your focus from the external response to the internal fulfillment that comes from touching someone's heart or sparking their imagination through your photographs.

Mindfully curate your images before sharing. Choose photographs that resonate with you on a deep level and evoke emotions or narratives that you find meaningful. Select images that authentically represent your unique perspective and experiences. As you curate, be mindful of the stories your photographs tell and the feelings they may evoke in others.

When the time comes to share your work, do so with a sense of presence and attentiveness. Write captions that provide insight into the emotions, thoughts, or stories behind the photographs. Share your intentions and reflections, inviting viewers to engage with the images on a deeper level. Use your words mindfully, crafting them with authenticity and vulnerability.

As you share your photographs, let go of attachment to the outcome. Release any expectations of how your work will be received or perceived. Instead, embrace the act of sharing as an opportunity to connect with others, inspire conversations, and cultivate a sense of community. Be open to the diverse responses and interpretations that your photographs may evoke.

Engage with your audience mindfully. Respond to comments and messages with gratitude and genuine interest. Seek to understand the impact your photographs have on others and create a space for meaningful dialogue. Approach conversations with empathy and respect, fostering connections that go beyond superficial likes or compliments.

Practice non-attachment to the metrics of social media or external validation. Instead of measuring the worth of your photographs by the number of likes or followers, focus on the quality of the connections and the impact your work has on individuals. Remember that even if your photographs touch just one person's heart, it is a meaningful and valuable contribution.

Embrace feedback and constructive criticism with an open mind. View it as an opportunity for growth and learning, rather than a judgment of your worth as a photographer. Mindfully consider the feedback and reflect on how it aligns with your intentions and artistic vision. Use it as a tool to refine your skills and further develop your unique voice.

Finally, engage in mindful reflection after sharing your photographs. Take time to process your own emotions and experiences, and reflect on the connections and conversations that have emerged. Appreciate the impact your work has had, both on others and on your own growth as a photographer and as a mindful individual.

Learning mindfulness and meditation can be enriched by sharing your photographs mindfully, with the intention to inspire and connect with others. Approach the act of sharing with consciousness and awareness, curating your images and crafting captions mindfully. Let go of attachment to external validation and focus on the connections and conversations that your work sparks. Embrace feedback with openness and gratitude, using it as a tool for growth. Ultimately, by sharing your photographs mindfully, you contribute to the well-being of others and create a meaningful impact through your creative expression.

Embrace Monochrome

Black and white photography strips away the distractions that color can bring, allowing you to concentrate on the fundamental elements of a scene. When you engage in black and white photography, pay close attention to the interplay of light and shadow, as they shape the form and texture of your subjects. Notice how different angles and perspectives can enhance the contrast and create a sense of depth.

As you immerse yourself in the process of capturing black and white photographs, cultivate a sense of curiosity and exploration. Experiment with different compositions, emphasizing shapes, lines, and patterns. By focusing on these elements, you train your mind to be present and attentive to the details that may go unnoticed in a color photograph.

With black and white photography, you have the opportunity to evoke and convey emotions in a powerful way. Embrace the moodiness, the simplicity, and the timeless quality that black and white images can possess. Pay attention to the emotional impact of your subjects, and experiment with different tonal ranges to enhance the desired mood and atmosphere.

To truly learn mindfulness and meditation through black and white photography, approach the process with a mindset of contemplation and reflection. Slow down and take your time to observe and connect with your subjects. Notice the subtle nuances and intricacies that can be revealed through shades of gray. By cultivating a sense of presence and stillness, you can create photographs that reflect the depth of your own experiences and perceptions.

Black and white photography also offers an opportunity to appreciate the beauty of simplicity. By removing the distraction of color, you can focus on the fundamental elements of a composition, distilling it down to its essential essence. Seek out minimalistic scenes or isolated subjects that convey a sense of quietude and balance. Embrace the power of negative space and the way it can enhance the visual impact of your photographs.

As you delve into black and white photography, study the works of renowned black and white photographers for inspiration. Notice how they use tones, contrast, and composition to create compelling and evocative images. Allow their work to inform and shape your own artistic vision, while still honoring your unique perspective and experiences.

To fully immerse yourself in the process of learning mindfulness and meditation through black and white photography, dedicate specific moments to review and reflect on your images. Take the time to examine each photograph and notice the emotions, thoughts, and sensations they evoke within you. Use these moments of reflection as opportunities for self-awareness and growth, allowing your photographs to serve as a mirror for your own inner world.

Exploring black and white photography can be a powerful tool for learning mindfulness and meditation. Embrace the absence of color and focus on the form, texture, and emotion of your subjects. Cultivate a sense of curiosity, contemplation, and reflection as you capture and review your images. Allow black and white photography to deepen your connection to the present moment, enhance your awareness, and inspire your creative expression.

Seek Reflections

Mindfulness and meditation can be deepened by seeking out reflective surfaces and capturing reflections in your photographs. Reflections have a unique ability to create intriguing and contemplative images that invite the viewer to explore their own perceptions and thoughts. By consciously engaging with reflective surfaces, you can cultivate a sense of presence, observation, and self-reflection.

When you are out photographing, keep an eye out for reflective surfaces such as still bodies of water, windows, mirrors, or polished surfaces. These surfaces offer a visual canvas that can transform ordinary scenes into captivating compositions. Approach them with a curious and open mind, as each reflection holds the potential to reveal hidden beauty and unique perspectives.

As you come across reflective surfaces, take a moment to pause and observe. Allow yourself to fully immerse in the present moment, noticing the interplay between the subject and its reflection. Observe how the reflection interacts with its surroundings, distorting or enhancing the perception of reality. By immersing yourself in this observation, you deepen your connection to the present and heighten your awareness of the intricacies of the moment.

When photographing reflections, consider the composition and framing of your image. Experiment with different angles and perspectives to capture the reflection in a way that is visually interesting and thought-provoking. Play with the symmetry or asymmetry that reflections can offer, creating a dynamic balance between the subject and its mirrored counterpart. Use the reflection as a compositional element to guide the viewer's eye and create a sense of depth.

Reflective surfaces also provide an opportunity for self-reflection and introspection. As you capture reflections, allow yourself to connect with the emotions and thoughts that arise within you. Notice how the reflection may mirror your own inner landscape or reflect aspects of your surroundings.

Use this process as a way to cultivate self-awareness and explore your own perceptions and perspectives.

To learn mindfulness and meditation through capturing reflections, approach the process with a sense of curiosity and mindfulness. Be fully present in the act of photographing, paying attention to the details and subtleties of the reflection. Allow yourself to let go of distractions and immerse yourself in the beauty and intrigue of the moment.

After capturing your images, take time for reflection and contemplation. Review each photograph and notice the emotions, thoughts, and sensations they evoke within you. Allow the reflection to serve as a metaphor for your own inner journey and invite introspection and self-inquiry. Use the images as a starting point for meditation and self-reflection, allowing them to guide you deeper into the present moment and your own inner world.

Seeking out reflective surfaces and capturing reflections in your photographs can be a powerful tool for learning mindfulness and meditation. Embrace the opportunity to observe and engage with the interplay between the subject and its reflection. Experiment with composition and framing to create visually intriguing images. Use reflections as a catalyst for self-reflection and introspection, deepening your connection to the present moment and your own inner landscape. By incorporating reflections into your photographic practice, you can enhance your mindfulness journey and cultivate a deeper sense of awareness and presence.

Document Daily Rituals

Capturing the beauty of your daily rituals and routines, allows you to find mindfulness in the mundane aspects of life. Often, we overlook the simple moments and activities that make up our daily lives, but through photography, we can cultivate a deeper sense of appreciation and presence in these ordinary moments.

Start by bringing awareness to your daily rituals and routines. Whether it's brewing a cup of coffee, preparing a meal, or engaging in personal care, these activities can become opportunities for mindfulness. Slow down and observe the details—the textures, colors, and shapes that make up these routines. Notice the sensations in your body, the scents in the air, and the sounds around you. By consciously engaging your senses, you can bring a heightened awareness to the present moment.

When photographing your daily rituals, approach them with a sense of curiosity and exploration. Experiment with different angles, perspectives, and compositions to capture the essence of the moment. Look for interesting details or patterns that might go unnoticed in the busyness of everyday life. By focusing on these elements, you bring attention to the present and discover the beauty that exists within the seemingly mundane.

One of the keys to learning mindfulness and meditation through capturing daily rituals is to cultivate a sense of gratitude and appreciation. Use your camera as a tool to express gratitude for the simple joys and moments that often pass by unnoticed. By directing your attention to these small moments, you can shift your perspective and find joy in the present. Notice the textures of the objects you interact with, the warmth of the light that illuminates your space, or the patterns that emerge as you engage in your routines. By appreciating these details, you deepen your connection to the present moment and cultivate a sense of gratitude.

Through photographing your daily rituals, you can also

develop a deeper understanding of the concept of impermanence. Notice how each moment is fleeting and ever-changing. By capturing these moments with your camera, you create a visual reminder of the impermanence of life. This awareness can bring a sense of mindfulness and appreciation for the transitory nature of our experiences.

Incorporating mindfulness into your daily rituals also involves being fully present in the act of photographing. Take your time to compose each shot, paying attention to the details and subtleties. Allow yourself to become fully absorbed in the process, letting go of distractions and thoughts about the past or future. By immersing yourself in the present moment, you heighten your ability to observe and appreciate the beauty that surrounds you.

After capturing your images, take moments for reflection and contemplation. Look back at the photographs and notice the emotions and sensations they evoke within you. Use these images as anchors for meditation or as reminders to bring mindfulness into your daily life. Allow them to serve as gentle reminders to find joy and appreciation in the simple moments and routines that make up your day.

Capturing the beauty of your daily rituals and routines can be a powerful way to learn mindfulness and meditation. By bringing awareness to these moments, you cultivate a deeper sense of appreciation and presence in your daily life. Use your camera as a tool to explore and celebrate the details and patterns that make up these routines. Practice gratitude and embrace the impermanence of each moment. By engaging in this mindful photography practice, you create a pathway to finding mindfulness in the mundane and discovering the beauty that exists within your everyday experiences.

About the Author

Skip Armstrong is an author who has created several books on a wide range of topics that provide readers with practical and inspiring information to help them lead a fulfilling and enjoyable life. His passion for producing valuable content stems from his desire to share knowledge and experience with others.

Skip Armstrong earned his degree in Study of Religion and Philosophy from the University of Northern Iowa. During his studies, he developed a keen interest in personal growth, and self-awareness, which he has since translated into writing. He believes that every individual has the potential to live a fulfilling life and that it is never too late to start the journey towards self-improvement.

In his books, Skip Armstrong draws upon his knowledge and experience to provide practical advice and guidance to readers. He has a knack for breaking down complex topics into simple, actionable steps, making his books accessible to a broad range of readers.

Through his work, Skip Armstrong has helped countless individuals take control of their lives and achieve their goals.

In his freetime, he enjoys playing the ukulele and guitar. He enjoys artistic expression, and philosophy. He asserts that finding joy in life through passions is the key to a healthy lifestyle.

He continues to enjoy creating new books, and learning more about the world as a whole. With such a short existence, there is much to take in!

Printed in Great Britain
by Amazon

49180612R00077